ACTING ON YOUR DREAMS & VISIONS

BY: KOFI PIESIE/ SEANATHAN POLIDORE /DR ASHELY WADE

© Same Tree Different Branch Publishing

Kofi Piesie/Seanathan Polidore/Dr. Ashley Wade

Copyright 2024 by Same Tree Different Branch Publishing

All rights reserved. No Part of this book may be reproduced or transmitted in any form or by any means, electronic or mechanical, including photocopying, recordings, or information storage and retrieval systems, without the publisher's written permission.

Printed in the United States of America

ISBN 979-8-9896372-8-7

Respect The Brands
STRIVING FOR GREATNESS

Table of Contents

Foreword – D. Lewis..................................5

Introduction – Keith J. Nickerson......................13

Prologue 1: Dream Chaser by Seanathan Polidore..21

Prologue 2: Kill the Fear! by Kofi Piesie............29

Prologue 3: Understand More and Fear Less by Dr. Ashley Wade..35

Chapter 1: Discovering the Power of Your Inner Vision by Kofi Piesie..................................41

Chapter 2: Turning Dreams into Goals by Seanathan Polidore..49

Chapter 3 Overcoming Obstacles, Fear, and Embracing Change: by Kofi Piesie..................59

Chapter 4: Harnessing Your Creativity and Innovation by Seanathan Polidore..................69

Chapter 5: Building Resilience and Persistence by Dr. Ashley Wade..81

Chapter 6: Celebrating Success and Reflecting on the Journey by Dr. Ashley Wade......................86

Chapter 7: Steps by Step Dreams, Goals, and Action Plan by Kofi Piesie..91

FOREWORD

Foreword

By D. Lewis

I would like to first thank Kofi Piesie, Sean P., and Dr. Wade for reaching out to me with this wonderful opportunity to pen the forward for this literary gem. I am eternally grateful that the three of you considered me a good addition to your masterpiece. It is truly my honor to call the three of you my Family.

Let us start our conversation by defining the words dream and vision. According to the Oxford Language Dictionary, the word dream has two definitions. 1.) a series of thoughts, images, and sensations that occur in a person's mind during sleep. 2.) a cherished aspiration, ambition, or ideal. Oxford Language Dictionary defines Vision as 1.) the faculty or state of being able to see. 2.) the ability to think about or plan the future with imagination or wisdom. For this conversation, I would like to focus on the second definition of both words.

Most of us experience at some point in our childhood or young adolescence what I like to refer to as the killing of dreams. As children, we've all had ambitions, ideas, and aspirations of what we wanted our lives to look like. However, the world around us quickly changed, and we started to hear phrases like, "Life is not a fairytale; you need to get serious about life and grow up." Or maybe we were told, "It's ok to dream, but they need to be more realistic, something more attainable." So, armed with that professional advice, we abandon our dreams and enter what is known as the "real world." Work, eat, sleep, rinse, and repeat. If we're lucky, we even get a chance to have a little fun thrown in there somewhere.

But I'm here to tell you that this is not the end of the story. Why? Because we still have the ability to dream. The biggest difference now is that we have complete autonomy in our lives. We no longer have to listen to what someone else thinks we should be doing. We can do as we please. This is where the real magical journey begins. When combined and used properly, dreams and vision(s) have the ability to shape our own individual reality in ways that we never imagined.

Today, Albert Einstein and Nikola Tesla are widely regarded as two of the greatest minds in modern history. The recognition they receive today for their contributions is in stark juxtaposition of what people thought of them when they were alive. They were said to be crazed men. Both men have profound quotes that have greatly affected many individuals' lives once understood. Let us first look at Einstein.

Einstein is quoted as saying, "The universe is mental." What Einstein is telling us here is that everything around us first had its beginning in the mind of someone. In short, someone had to dream of it, and that dream turned into a vision of what it would look like, how it would function, etc... Wherever you are right now, take a look around. The floor, the table, the cup, the paper this book is written on, the house, the car, the walls, carpet, lights, television, and computer, all of it first had to be an ideal, ambition, or aspiration in the mind of someone; it was their dream. Then, they imagined it existing. Think for a second about all the things we take for granted today that may not have existed if someone never allowed themselves to dream of it.

Now, we take a look at Tesla. Tesla is quoted as saying, "If you wish to understand the universe, think in terms of energy." Simply put, everything is energy. All the aforementioned items are simply atoms, molecules, protons, and electrons repurposed to form different things. The only difference is the rate of speed at which they move. The key word here is MOVE. The dream and vision of something must have some force, action, or movement in conjunction with it to bring that dream/vision to fruition. It really is a simple formula. We have the ideas (dream), then we see the dream within our mind(envision), and then our emotions compel us to act in alignment with the vision (we work toward it). This is the true magic which every human being has the ability to use in order to create the life they really want.

I'll share my own experience with you. At around age 43 (I'm 47 now), I was at somewhat of a crossroads in my life. After spending many years in corporate management, I decided to leave. I was initially anxious, but that turned into excitement when I realized I could do whatever I wanted now. However, the issue quickly arose that I had absolutely no clue of what I wanted to do or what I even liked to do. You see, I had spent my entire adult life doing what other people wanted or what I thought others expected of me. I had truly lost myself. After a brief period of depression, I started my quest to figure out who I really was. The process was pretty intense and sometimes downright scary, but I emerged from it with an entirely different outlook on my life.

During this time, a good friend approached me to produce an audiobook for a book they had written. Now, for all the turning new leaf talk and being open to change, I would be a bold-faced lie if I did not tell you that I was adamantly against this idea. I had never done anything close to this before in my life. I didn't know where to start. Plus, I don't have a good enough voice for it. Fortunately for me, my wife lovingly and forcefully encouraged me to go for it. More importantly, I actually listened to her. I found that I actually enjoyed it, and it was kind of good. I then thought of the possibility of this working out for me. Soon after, I envisioned being a full-time voice actor and living life on my own terms. I began auditioning for other jobs, and to my surprise, I got them. Today, I am no longer auditioning for most of my work; people are requesting me to produce their projects. I realized there is a world of possibilities out there for me to take this thing wherever my heart desires. All I have to do is continue refining the dream, envisioning the details, and putting in the work to manifest itself in my life.

This book is comprised by three individuals who are truly living their lives like a dream and on their own terms. I truly enjoy how the information is laid out in a step-by-step, cohesive manner that is easy to follow and understand. They share with you how to regain your power to dream and protect those dreams from individuals who may want to sabotage them. They share their own experiences of how to nurture those dreams into visions and set active goals to bring and keep yourself in alignment with them. Also they share how to avoid pitfalls and how to handle perceived setbacks, as well as how to celebrate the success of not only achieving your ultimate goal but also the milestones along the way. If you are searching for answers on finding your personal power as a creator, this book is written primarily for you.

-D. Lewis, The Narrator

INTRODUCTION

Introduction

By Keith J. NICKERSON

My input in this collaborative project is to rekindle the essence of suggestion, re-acquainting readers to what exists within. An inauguration does not transpire in a formal setting; instead, it's a prelude to creativity in real time, in the mind. Allowing introspection promotes self-discovery, and in the correct environment and properly nourished potential once internally dormant manifests into actual fruits of completion.

"NOBODY CAN BE YOU BUT YOU!"

Desire burns within us all; tap into it; stop talking about it and be about it. I can't introduce anyone to Dreams and Visions generated in their deepest recesses. That's a 1-on-1, private, intimate experience; acknowledge those bold enough to share their mental fantasies; society labels them as trailblazers and precedence setters. No one knows what smolders internally, and it remains in anonymity unless the wick is re-lit. Concepts rooted within, once put on display, allow all of humanity to witness your genius, recognizing that special "IT" factor you possess.

"WHO'S DREAMS & VISIONS, ARE THEY?"

Private, personal thoughts and ideas constantly flood the conscious and subconscious minds. Momentary imaginations rudely snapped out of, disrupted daydreams, and sadly unable to return to that exact spot or moment in time. Sharing glimpses of places mentally whisked off to, precursors of what's to come, or reliving past interactions, days of old. The remembrances generating perplexing ponderance of:

WHO, WHAT, WHEN, and WHERE?

Have no fear, dare to be, to do, to try, to fail, and success isn't far behind. Our Higher Power, in its infinite wisdom, formed

_____!!!! Believe in yourself; that's the most difficult step of the journey. Boldly stand and embrace your difference; the essence of **LIFE** is the culmination/reaching of Dreams & Visions. I have no crystal ball, nor can I share a specific earth-shaking incident which formed the present man. Dreams & Visions exist in the future realm, a road paved by innovative thinkers like yourself:

DREAMERS & VISIONARIES
NELSON MANDELA

"Our deepest fear is not that we are inadequate. Our deepest fear is that we are powerful beyond measure. It's our light, not our darkness, that most frightens us. We ask ourselves, who am I to be brilliant, gorgeous, talented, or fabulous; actually, who are you not to be? You are a child of God, and you playing small doesn't serve the world. There's nothing enlightening about shrinking so other people won't feel insecure around you. We were born to manifest the glory of God that's within. It's not just in some; it's in everyone. When we let our light shine, we unconsciously give other people our permission to do the same. As we are liberated from our own fear, our presence automatically liberates others."

"BEFORE YOU CAN ACHIEVE IT, YOU HAVE TO DREAM/ENVISION IT."

Dreams and Visions transpire both day and night, whether awake or asleep, intended, or unintended. Stored within each of us is a vast file of blank moments and drifts; hidden within lies creativity. Once defused by inequality, discouraged through glass ceiling limitations, and destroyed by pigeon-holed thinkers, precedence setters went unseen. Mental imagination can occur with eyes wide open and clear minds.

"DREAM BIG AND FOLLOW THEM, THEY KNOW THE WAY."

Take a few moments to recall a few commonly shared scenarios:

1) Recall the little girl/boy in you seated at the kitchen table; it's your birthday. A cake with lit candles is in front of you, and mom, dad, sisters, brothers, etc. suggest:

"Close your eyes and make a **WISH!**"

2) The little altar boy who wants to buy a new pair of Chuck Taylor Converse All-Stars but has only .37¢ in his piggy bank. Tonight, in a dark, quiet room, on his knees, he'll **PRAY** to a Higher Power.

What are his **PRAYERS**?

3) After watching a movie with family, the young teenage couple is allowed some private time. No chaperone, finally alone, holding hands, they walk down the sidewalk. Both shy and slowly beginning to break down barriers of inhibition and inexperience, they gaze into the dark night. A sudden streak of light flashed through the darkness, a falling star.

What do both privately **ENVISION**?

Impressionable in youth, way back then, someone or something caught your eye; what was "**IT**"? Actions or a style so uniquely different, witnessing it sent your imagination on a trip. That sunny, bright Saturday afternoon, relaxing in the backyard after watching Soul Train, you discovered why your caged bird fears singing. Buck the norm, refrain from the latest social media trend, be that Raisin in the Sun, and try living from the mind. Thought interpretation is enlightening, prompting self-growth. The entirety of LIFE, if blessed to possess a healthy, rational mind, it's the source of ideas initially seeded by Dreams and Visions. Pray the flow never ceases, never stop Dreaming; if you do, a part of your inner DIES. Always aspire; it's an unquenchable fire.

"MY DAY ISN'T RIGHT, UNLESS I WRITE!"

HEBREWS 11:1

"FAITH IS THE SUBSTANCE OF THINGS HOPED FOR, THE EVIDENCE OF THINGS NOT SEEN."

SO ARE DREAMS!!!!!

PROLOGUE 1

Seanathan Polidore

Dream Chaser

Seanathan Polidore

"Dreams come a size too big so we can grow into them" by Josie Bisse

In our last publication, The Modern-Day Griot, I told you about the academic struggles I experienced as a young boy of the 80s, and I led you to my eventual transformation into an avid reader and multi-published author. In this story, I want to take you through a different aspect of my childhood that played an essential role in me becoming the man that I am today. Let me take you back to that same trailer in Franklin, LA. I am about three or four years of age. Our floor model T.V. is blasting, and I am engulfed in Kung Fu theater. Like most children of my era, I was so in love with martial arts. Bruce Lee, Van Damn, Bruce Leroy, Steven Siguel, you name an action star at that time, and I wanted to analyze them twenty-four hours a day. When I think about what most of my peers wanted to be as kids, it was cops, firefighters, ball players, and doctors, but when it came to me, I wanted to be a ninja! I know it sounds funny to say it out loud, but this was the first time I can recall having a dream and a vision about something. When the other young boys around me were playing basketball, baseball, and football, you could find me in the backyard practicing kicks and backflips until the streetlight came on. For some reason, I remember this moment going to my mother the way an innocent child does, and I said, Momma, I want to be a Ninja! She looked at me with that megawatt smile that she has, and she merely says OK. That one word, two letters. It meant so much to me subconsciously, I suppose. I just knew I had the full license to try with all my might to be a ninja, and it was fine because my mother said so. It had to be true because, to a child, a mother would never tell you something that wasn't so, right? From that moment forward, I remember my mom putting me into local martial classes, allowing me to compete in a karate tournament, and buying me every Black Belt magazine I begged for in the magazine aisle of the local stores. She did everything she could with the resources we had to show me she supported my dream and actively backed it for as long as I had it.

When you are a child, a lot of us pick up things and sit them down eventually. At around nine years old, I decided to put down the ninja stars and nunchaku and picked up a basketball. Basketball in the 90s was what some today would call the golden age of the game. Micheal Jordan was flying high, Shawn Kemp (my favorite player) was bringing the Rain with the Supersonics, and Shaq was taking the league by storm. I have a wild idea; yeah, I have a brand-new dream: I want to play basketball. So, this time, I would take my dream to my grandfather and ask him if it would be possible to get me a basketball goal for the front yard. It took some good old begging and pleading, but my grandparents always spoiled me, and eventually, he surprised me with a brand-new basketball goal and covered our shell rock yard with concrete. Again, I was allowed to dream and the space to dream as wildly and widely as I could imagine. From that moment on, throughout my childhood, I could be found day and night pounding the rubber off the ball. My dreams became more vivid at this age. As I said in the Modern-day Griot chapter, my hoop dream was so large I couldn't even focus on my classes. I wasn't thinking about anything else in this world for years besides that ball. The way I dressed, walked, talked, and every inch of my room was about the dream. Again, my family fueled my dream by sending me to Grambling University camps in the summer, allowing me to play in various leagues around the city, and letting me venture far and wide on my own to find guys to play with. All of these actions and more were their forms of allowing me to grow and develop the love and passion for this game that just came over me out of the blue one day. They never tried to throw water on my flames that burned white hot at that critical stage in my life.

I'll flash forward to my adulthood to make it all come full circle for you. The basketball dreams didn't pan out exactly like I wanted, but from the martial arts and basketball journey, I knew that if I put my mind to something and was willing to put in the work, my dreams could be reachable. They were worth going for with all the might I could muster, and more importantly, I knew that even if the idea didn't work, I always had people behind me, ready to catch me and put me back on my feet when I needed it. You see dreams occur while you are asleep, and your support system becomes your favorite pillow. Even in my 30s, I would go to my mother and say I want to start my gym; she would say well, ok. Hey ma, I think I want to go to college now; she says ok. Hey ma, guess what? I think I want to write my first book, and she says ok. You know what, ma, I think I can do this public speaking thing and interview guests, of course, she echos ok. There isn't any hair-brain idea I would think that would make me feel as if it was impossible and too out of reach to at least attempt it because of the continued support of my family and friends throughout my life.

I know every person's background and family structure is different. Maybe you are reading my story and can't relate to it for one bit. Perhaps you feel as if you never had support in your life for anything you ever dreamed of. I want to encourage you and inspire you to go out and seek new people to be that support you need to add fuel to your fire for your goals. If you happen to be in the sports world like I was as a young man, my coaches, and sensei were amazing additional supports for me during that vital point in my development. If you have different types of dreams, look toward the staff at the school you attend, or maybe some upstanding people in your community could point you toward someone they may know who is in the field that you are curious about. Lastly, nothing beats this information age that we are sitting in currently. Online allows us to reach out to literally billions of people from our phones or laptops quickly, easily, and cost-effectively. Luckily for you, we are no longer confined to the people living within driving distance of us. We can find groups, chat rooms, or entire universes online that are within the realm of the dream we have in our hearts. These are spaces where people are just as crazy about a particular topic as you are, and most of them don't mind sharing their tricks of the trade if you ask. Nothing comes to a sleeper but a dream. Please go out and do something with it.

Sean P.

Acts 2:17: In the End Times, many believers will see dreams.

PROLOGUE 2

Kofi Piesie

Kill the Fear!

(By Kofi Piesie)

African Proverb (Ethiopia): One cannot stop sleeping because of the fear of bad dreams.

Meaning: The fact that there is the tendency to be choked by food does not mean you should not eat. Just because there is the risk of failure does not mean you should not pursue success. Everything in life is a risk. To try is a risk and not to try is also a risk. So, weigh both options to see which one is in your best interest. Don't let the fear of failure rob you of any good thing in life.

I have been around the sun 46 times and heard through half of those 46 years people talking about their visions and dreams. Most of the conversations I had with those individuals were just talk. They never acted on their vision and dreams because of fear, laziness, and discouragement from them, letting their friends and family talk them out of their vision and dreams. Let me say this: You have to be careful when telling others your vision because they will push their own insecurities and fears off on you and talk you right out of it. No one sees or believes in your vision and dreams more than you do. Again, I repeat, be careful when sharing, and in my opinion, why share with someone who is not doing anything, who does not have a good work ethic, someone who is a complainer, and one who is always negative. I suggest you find someone who had a similar vision and executed their vision and dreams in the physical in real-time. Reach out for advice and ask if they could mentor you. Surround yourself with people who are positive and who can be an inspiration in your life to push you and believe you can achieve everything in that vision and dream.

I want to tell a quick story about me that happened way back. I cannot remember a time when I was not creative and envisioned myself doing everything, I was good at and succeeding. You can say I have always been a dreamer. As I dream this and envision that, I can say there was always fear in my mind that stopped me from acting on them. I'll talk about how I overcame the fear in the moment but let me share one story where I wanted to start an organization for local recording artists and surrounding artists in the area. This musical organization would help us all by having money to put on our own shows and travel from state to state. The goal was to make us more noticeable to where major record labels or prominent investors could see us. The goal was also to buy equipment or more state-of-the-art equipment and build a studio or use someone spot to house the equipment so that we could record, mix, and package up our own CDs. In order for it to work, we needed at least 20 musical artists. Each artist would pay a hundred dollars dues a month. In 6 months, we could have acquired twelve thousand dollars or, in twelve months, twenty-four thousand. That money would go toward a few of our shows, which would get all of us noticed more locally and in surrounding areas. Plus, doing the show, we could charge a small fee to make some of our money back. The money would also help us get the recording software we needed. I thought it was a good idea, and at that time, that was my dream and vision, which was we recording artists would create an organization that would help us all in the long run. I ran my vision past a few friends and family members, and all I heard was ah, man, that isn't going to work. Nobody is going to put in a hundred dollars per month, or what about if no one shows up to you all shows blah, blah blah continues. With me not having a lot of confidence and having that fear, I let friends and a family member talk me right out of trying to get the organization off the ground and reaching out to the many artists who were doing music. I have many stories after that where fear set in, and I allowed others to talk me out of acting on my visions and dreams.

My fear didn't leave until I joined a Masonic Lodge in 2006. The lodge I am referring to is Hattiesburg Lodge #165. There were a lot of intelligent and confident men in that lodge. As I began to study and read all the time, I gained some responsibility in the lodge, and that's when I began to have confidence in myself, and I changed my life by just acting on it. I love studying and being responsible for teaching new brothers who join the lodge. Later, I started having visions of being the head officer, which means being in charge. That happened three years later because I envisioned it and saw the vision through by working the steps I needed to get elected into that head seat. The confidence, the work ethic, and the not entertaining the not-so-positive feedback about that not going working, that's a one million shot, you got to know somebody that knows somebody spill. I would cut the conversation quickly. I would always surround myself around positive people who was smarter than me.

Before I end the prologue, never be afraid to try; never be afraid to reach out to others who have made their dreams come true. If you are a dreamer or a visioner, I say act now and kill the fear! This book will further explain and guide you in the direction of acting on your visions and your dreams.

PROLOGUE 3

Dr. Ashley Wade

Understand More and Fear Less

Dr. Ashley Wade

"Nothing in life is to be feared; it's only to be understood. Now is the time to understand more and fear less." Marie Curie

Good People,

This quote above is one of my favorite quotes because, to me, the message is: Life is about Learning and Paying attention. We have been conditioned to believe that, at some point, we should stop learning because we know so much. This is why there are a lot of people who are stagnant in their lives. They want more and hope for better, but they choose to fear instead of understanding.

I knew when I was a sophomore in high school that I wanted to one day be a pharmacist. I was so inspired by my chemistry class and my attentive teacher that I made up my mind that very year (way back when.) So, I went on a voyage with that aspiration in mind. Besides having an intensive chemistry/biology background, you must take a pharmacy entrance exam and do an in-person interview. I was terrified of both of the latter requirements. And that fear was Justified- in my mind. The PCAT is a very difficult entrance exam; my first 3 times taking the test, I scored unfavorably. The 4th time I took the test, my score wasn't great, but it landed me an interview at a pharmacy school that interested me. I was super nervous, but I attended the interview, and I was utterly intimidated sitting across from 2 older white men as a young black woman seeking not only to further my education but to move up in the tax bracket (know what I'm talmbout?) This interview was one of the worst experiences in my life. Those gatekeepers were completely judgmental because, at that point, I had been out of college for some years. The starkest question was, what makes you think you'll be successful in our program since you've been out of school for 5 years? Ugh. Needless to say, I didn't get accepted and then crept in worry and fear. What if I had chosen a career that I could never obtain? Self-doubt: maybe I won't be successful in a doctorate program. I was completely bummed. After this situation, I had the opportunity to tutor science at a charter school, which led to me teaching an AP chemistry class. This is when I had the epiphany. My inspiration came from my 10th-grade chemistry class, and now I'm teaching a 10th-grade chemistry class. I realized that maybe there was something I needed to do here before I could elevate. What lesson was there to be learned? What more could I UNDERSTAND about this pit stop? Could I use the skills I acquired while teaching for my future career? Once I started to put the pieces together, you'll never believe how my life started to change. I began looking at other things from a different lens. The next time I took the PCAT, my score improved so greatly that I was confident I could get accepted to any school I applied for…. And that came true! I got accepted to every school that I applied to (I sure did), and now it was up to me to make a decision on the College of Pharmacy that was the best fit for me. No longer did I have to settle. Not only that, but those public speaking and teaching skills that I picked up were instrumental in my 3rd-year Recitation classes, where I presented patient cases in front of a resident and my peers. I was actually ahead of the game in that respect.

Fast forward, I earned my Doctorate of Pharmacy in 2016, and I've practiced in the retail setting; now, I work as a consultant pharmacist for a mail-order company.

I shared this part of my story to demonstrate how important it is to seek to understand. I'll never tell anyone not to be afraid because that's a part of human nature, but don't let fear paralyze you on your Journey. Look around for clues, connections, and your path. It Will unfold if you work with life. The perceived setback may actually be a challenge to your drive and character. There's likely a lesson in the challenge. How will you know if you're resilient if you aren't tested? How courageous are you? How much do you Believe in Yourself? How often do you look for alignment in the events in your life? The lessons? Do you pay attention to how the Universe is working in Your Favor?

I hope that as you read this book, you keep an open mind about who you are as a person and receive these valuable gems from our experiences to your psyche and, ultimately, your Elevation.

WE. GROW. TOGETHER.

Peace and Blessings,

Dr. Ashley Wade

Pharmacist, Author, Community and Literacy Advocate, Curator, Griotte.

CHAPTER 1

Kofi Piesie

Chapter One

"Discovering the Power of Your Inner Vision"

By Kofi Piesie

In a world full of dreams and aspirations, taking action is the key to success. Whether you dream of becoming a basketball or football star, a musician, a teacher, starting your own business, or transforming the world with your innovative ideas, acting on your dreams and vision sets you apart from the rest. It's about turning your imagination into reality and making a positive impact in your life and the lives of others. Let's look at the word imagination and define its meaning.

Imagination

1. the faculty or action of forming new ideas, images, or concepts of external objects not present to the senses.

2. the ability of the mind to be creative or resourceful.

3. the part of the mind that imagines things.

(Oxford Online Dictionary)

My imagination is always running wild with ideas. This is why I walk around with a small composition book in my side or back pocket. I do not sleep much, but when I sleep, my imagination is going in my dreams so to speak. This is also why I keep a notepad by my bed to jot down the ideas I envision in my dreams when I wake up. My imagination runs wild when driving, going to dinner with the family, at work, watching TV, and in my home office. As I mentioned, I keep a small composition book in my pocket, so I'll pull it out at any given time and start writing down what is on my mind. Imagination is the process of the mind. After writing, I would read it back and envision manifesting those things, creating and producing those ideas from my imagination. It is the same way if I wake up from a Dream; I write it down and then have a vision. Imagination occurs when one is conscious, and Dreams occur when one is usually in a state of sleep. Both are ways of using creativity. My day-to-day formal is Imagination x Dreams x Vision.

Dreams and Visions: To understand them better, let's look deeper into them.

Understanding Dreams and Visions

Dreams and visions are the fuel that ignites our passion and drives us forward. They are glimpses of what we truly desire, the images that inspire us to take action. Understanding the significance of dreams and visions is crucial to fully embracing their power.

Paragraph 1: Dreams are the manifestation of our deepest desires. They are the sparks of inspiration that guide us towards our true purpose. Dreams can be big or small, but they all have one thing in common - they hold the potential to change our lives. When we tap into our dreams, we tap into our true potential.

Paragraph 2: Visions, however, are the detailed images of what we want to achieve. They are the blueprints of our dreams, providing us with a clear direction and a sense of purpose. Visions help us to set specific goals and create a roadmap for success.

Paragraph 3: Dreams and visions go hand in hand. Dreams provide the inspiration, while Visions provide the focus. When we combine the power of both, we create a powerful force that propels us forward and keeps us motivated even in the face of challenges.

The Power of Dreams and Visions

Dreams and visions can transform our lives in ways we never thought possible. They are the driving force behind every outstanding achievement and the catalyst for personal growth and fulfillment.

Paragraph 1: Dreams and visions give us a reason to wake up excited and purposeful every morning. They give us a sense of direction and a clear path to follow. When we have a dream or a vision, we have something to work towards that gives our lives meaning.

Paragraph 2: Dreams and visions also have the power to inspire others. When we act on our dreams, we show others what is possible. We become a source of inspiration and motivation for those around us, encouraging them to pursue their own dreams and visions.

Paragraph 3: Dreams and visions can shape our reality. When we believe in our dreams and act toward them, we start attracting the resources, opportunities, and people we need to make them a reality. Our dreams become magnets that draw in everything we need to succeed.

Turning Dreams and Visions into Goals

Turning dreams and visions into goals is a topic I will touch on briefly because, in chapter two, my fellow Modern-Day Griot Seanathan Polidore will give you an in-depth chapter on transforming your dreams and visions into achievable goals, including setting clear objectives and creating a roadmap for success.

While dreams and visions are powerful, they can remain just fantasies if we don't turn them into actionable goals. Goals provide us with a roadmap and a plan of action to transform our dreams into reality.

Paragraph 1: The first step in turning dreams and visions into goals is to get clear on what you want to achieve. Take the time to visualize your dream and create a detailed vision of what it looks like. Please write, draw, or find images representing your vision. The more vivid and specific your vision, the easier it is to turn it into a goal.

Paragraph 2: Once you have a clear vision, break it down into smaller, more manageable goals. Create a step-by-step plan that outlines the actions you need to take to achieve each goal. Breaking your vision down into smaller goals makes it more achievable and less overwhelming.

Paragraph 3: Set deadlines for each goal and hold yourself accountable. Deadlines create a sense of urgency and motivate you to take action. Ensure your deadlines are realistic but challenging enough to push you outside your comfort zone.

Conclusion Let me reiterate that dreams and visions go hand in hand. Dreams provide inspiration, while visions provide the focus. Both are essential for pulling those ideas and images out of your mind and setting realistic goals. Stay focused, and never let anyone take your eyes off your vision. Your dreams and visions are yours, so keep that in mind when doubters and haters approach you. Let your dreams and vision be the drive that moves you forward. Unlock your full potential inside and use it to act on your Dreams. Throughout this book, you will see the word act. Act means to take action, and I want you to "act out" on your dreams and vision." "Act Out" simply means to translate something into action. That something is your dreams and vision, so take action and create goals and a step-by-step plan. Work on the plan and keep your eyes on the main objective, and even when you arrive and fulfill your dream, still keep your eye on that objective, stay focused, and take your dreams and vision to the moon and back.

CHAPTER 2

Seanathan Polidore

Chapter Two

Turning Dreams into Goals

(Seanathan Polidore)

"If I can see it in my mind, I can touch it with my hands."

Before I delve into the central focus of this chapter, I want to leave a special reminder for the reader. If you currently have a dream in your mind, you are a part of a small percentage of the population. Naturally, every person walking around us daily has a dream of some type. If you really think about most people at your job, school, community, and social interactions, this is not the case. Most of them are totally satisfied living the "hum drum" Lifestyle. They are comfortable clocking in and clocking out weekly from year to year in a place they don't necessarily care about. They are fine frequenting the same places and experience time and time again on repeat in a vicious cycle. I want to say that I am not talking down on anyone, and if that is your goal and that is how you define a great life, congratulations, more power to you. If you are reading this publication, I'm not imagining that being your idea of success. So, the simple fact is that you do have a burning desire in your chest that keeps you up at night. You feel emotions you can't explain every time you arrive at your occupation. You do have visions that go beyond your current surroundings. You are exceptional, and I don't care how crazy your family, friends, and coworkers think you are (we shall address them later).

Make It Plain

Now that the pat on the back portion of the book is out of the way, let's get down to the brass tax of taking those dreams out of your chest and making them manifest in your fingers. The first tried and true method of making your dreams real is to write them down! In my first book, What's Your Kick, I have a chapter about Reverse Engineering Your Goals. Check it out for a detailed explanation of how to use this concept. In short, I will tell you to write your goal down in as much vivid detail as possible for this book. What does it look, taste, sound, smell, and feel like? If you were to accomplish it, how would you feel instantly? Whatever your responses are to these questions, think about them deeply and record them. Next, I want you to work your way backward from that feeling to six months before that. What actions and habits would you need to start right now to end up with the feelings you experienced when you visualized the end game? How would your day-to-day life need to look? What things do you take part in now that you would have to remove yourself from? What group of people are taking from your energy and time and not adding to your result? Are there distractions in your life at this moment that you know are pulling you in the wrong direction than the one you claim you want to be on? Take your time, breathe, and step away from the book for a few moments. I want you to be brutally and painfully honest in your notes because the person that you are right now reading this and the person you saw in your mind are only separated by your ability to be disciplined in these areas in your life and applying what you are learning. This is the moment where old sages say that knowledge is not power, but applied knowledge is power. These books are never intended for you to read and feel warm and fuzzy about the words on the page; these books are action books. You know in your heart the answer to every question presented, but your strict application will prove you to be a wise master or a person whose dream was dried like a raisin in the sun. Make it so plain you can't miss.

Don't Turn Your Vision Board Into Painting with A Twist

I am sure by now most of us are familiar with the pastime known as painting with a twist. For those who don't know, painting with a twist is an outing where you and a group of friends and family go to a location. Most times, these events are led by an actual artist, and before the date arrives, the party's host has selected a particular picture she or he wants the group to paint. The instructor will have a canvas for every person present with an outline of the painting of the night. The instructor will curate the night, telling the party step by step what to do to turn their plain canvas into the desired picture. The twist in the title comes from the fact that most of the time, music plays while you paint, and you can indulge in your food and drink of choice. It really is a very fun evening, and if you have not gone, I highly advise it. Now, why would I mention painting with a twist in a book about dreams, you may be asking yourself at this point? Well, the sad thing about painting with a twist is that a lot of times, after a person has a great night out with the family and you take a group picture with your painting, you take that painting and stick it in the trunk of your car or the closet at your home never to see the light of day again. I don't want you to take your time creating vision boards and new year planning journals to stick them in a place where they will not be seen again. It would be best if you had your dreams in front of your face every day to keep you motivated and to stoke the flame inside of you until it becomes a raging flame. If you are an artist or a writer, have your vision board at your workstation so that every time your head pops up from your work, it's right there front and center, stirring at you. If you are an on-the-go, busybody type of person like me, take a picture of your vision board and save it as a screensaver on your phone, tablet, and laptop. You want to put direct pressure on yourself to fulfill the promise that you made for yourself at New Year's. It doesn't matter if you are a religious person or not. Holy water, oil, cross, rosary beads, sage, etc., never ever work unless you do. The same holds true with a vision board, planners, productivity apps, A.I. technology, or anything else man-made. They will never ever work unless you do! They are tools and enhancements, yes, but they were never created with the intent of being a substitute for hard work and discipline toward your goals.

I will conclude this portion with a very short personal story to drive home my point. Years ago, when I was writing my first book, I had an artist create the book cover for me way before the book came out. That cover became my phone and laptop screensaver. For six to eight months, every time I went to use either device, that amazing cover was there looking at me. I felt this sense of not wanting to have a cover of this beauty, not being seen by the world because of my procrastination or fear. This photo was the shot of adrenaline I needed to get over the finish line.

Tell the World

I know we live in a time where folks feel as if the world is full of people praying and wishing for your downfall. That type of thinking can make us feel as if we have to keep our dreams to ourselves for fear that someone is going to try to steal our ideas or they will throw ice water on our fire. I am here to tell you to let go of those false notions. One of the most motivating things that I have found is to be more public about the goals and dreams that I am pursuing. Once you make your dreams public, you now have a built-in accountability system. People will periodically ask you about the things you spoke about and posted months ago. They will want to know how it is coming along, is it still happening, when can they expect it? Etc. The idea of not having a great answer to these questions motivated me on the nights that I didn't feel like line editing at two in the morning. These questions made me accelerate sending the proper emails, phone calls, and letters to get my projects done versus spending weeks dragging my feet as if I had all the time in the world. I wanted to proudly and loudly say, hey, I am in the editing phase, or the book cover came back to me two weeks ago, and now we are going to print. Moments like this will give you the confidence and boldness to get your dreams done in ways you can't imagine, and when it's all said and done, you will be so glad that you chose to make it public compared to holding it close to your chest.

I want to add another benefit of being public about your goals. When you let people inside of what your ideas are, you never know who may have some connections, resources, or funding that could push your idea to a level you never thought of on your own. Never underestimate people around you, even strangers. The person you need to make that one phone call to get you into the room may pass right by you at the mall if your face is stuck in your phone. The connection you need to fund a community project could be that one guy at your job that you don't really feel all that good about. I'm presenting these examples because when I speak to teens at schools about making eye contact with strangers, having great manners, and speaking up to strangers, all of these things happen on a regular basis, but most of us don't pay enough attention to realize it's happening. Let this paragraph be your wake-up call right now to pay more attention to your surroundings and start telling people what you are pursuing. I don't care if they tell you, ok, we get it, keep going. Keep asking and keep bringing it up to anyone who will listen. When that one connection opens up for you, it will make the difference between you being in the game and watching it.

CHAPTER 3

Kofi Piesie

Chapter Three

Overcoming Obstacles, Fear, and Embracing Change

(Kofi Piesie)

In pursuing our dreams, we often face self-doubt and fear of external factors like financial constraints or unexpected life events. It's easy to lose confidence when faced with roadblocks and hardship, but it's important to remember that overcoming obstacles and embracing change are integral parts of the journey towards realizing our dreams. I discussed my fear in the prologue and shared my story and how I overcame the fear.

What is Fear?

Fear – 1. an unpleasant emotion caused by the belief that someone or something is dangerous, likely to cause pain or a threat.

2. be afraid of (someone or something) as likely to be dangerous, painful, or threatening.

Before I talk about identifying obstacles and embracing change, I want to share a quick Ethiopian folktale called "Conquering Fear." This folktale is about a young Ethiopian boy named Miobe who is shy and fearful of the world around him. One day, Miobe asks his grandfather why do you call me that? His Grandfather laughed and said because you are afraid," he answered. Your grandmother, mother, father, and neighbors all say the same thing.

Miobe thought carefully about what his grandfather said, and right then and there, he decided he must find a way to conquer fear and that night when everyone was fast asleep, he packed a sack and set off into the world to find out what he feared and to conquer it. As Miobe leaves his village and camps for the night, he was awaken by the howling of wolves. Instead of running away, he walked toward the sound, saying aloud, "I will conquer you, fear." He walked until the sun began to rise, and when he saw its golden orb, he smiled with relief, for he had survived the first night. "I am becoming brave," he said as he walked on. Later, he reached a village, and fear began to kick in; at that moment, he thought, "I don't know these people at all. They might be unkind to a stranger. But he straightened up and walked right into the village, saying aloud, "I will conquer you, fear." As Miobe approaches the village elders, they ask who you are. He replied, "I am Miobe, and I am traveling the world to become brave," he answered. The Elders laughed and muttered a few words. The Elders went on to explain that there was a monster on top of the mountain: "Our village is being threatened by a monster up on the mountain." Miobe followed the elderly men to the top of the mountain. At first, Miobe did not see a monster when elders said look, there is a monster. One elder after the next begins to describe the monster's features.

Now, Miobe began to see the monster. He began to see the smoke, fire, wrinkled skin, and fiery eyes. "I see," he said, but silently, he promised himself he would not be afraid. So, he walked away from the elders into the village proper. Miobe looked and saw how crops were untended to; children were not going to school in fear of the monster. Finally, Miobe decided it was up to him to destroy the monster. "I wish to conquer fear," he announced, "and so I shall go slay the monster!" The folktale goes on to say he climbed the mountain, and the further he got up, the smaller the giant monster began to look. To read the complete and detailed folktale, look at it.

Just like Miobe did, we must face our fears head-on. Once we do that, we begin to see those fears get smaller. That fear no longer looks like a giant fiery monster that is stopping you from going out into the world to share your dreams and visions by acting on them.

Let's discuss obstacles and how they can stress and make a person want to give up. I have had all kinds of obstacles in my life, and I can honestly say that fear and some barriers placed in my life made me quit pursuing anything I envisioned and dreams I had for myself and others. Obstacles stop me from seeing through a few businesses I have tried to get off the ground or keep. Some of the most rich and successful people have had obstacles in their way but didn't give up and kept going. They kept working and acting on their dreams and visions. People such as Bill Gates, who had failed business ventures where he didn't make any money from them; Oprah Winfrey, who had a bad childhood where her family was poor and was molested during her childhood and early teenage years and became pregnant at 14; her son was born prematurely and died in infancy. She faced many other challenges but pushed through and didn't give up. Jay Z, whom some refer to as the greatest rapper alive, but I don't share that same sentiment. Jay-Z had dreamed of being a rapper and getting a record deal. But his rise to stardom didn't happen overnight. He was faced with several roadblocks along the path to ultimate success. For example, in 1995, when Jay-Z tried tirelessly to strike a record deal, not a single label would sign him. It led him to establish his record company, Roc-a-fella Records, with partners Damon Dash and Kareem Biggs. Those obstacles, roadblocks, and setbacks didn't stop him from acting on his dreams and what he envisioned for himself.

Identifying the Obstacles

The first step in overcoming obstacles is to identify them. It's essential to be honest with yourself and acknowledge the fears, doubts, and external challenges that are holding you back. You can create a plan to address these obstacles effectively by pinpointing them.

1. Self-Doubt and Fear

Self-doubt and fear are common companions on the path to pursuing your dreams. The fear of failure, criticism, or the unknown can paralyze even the most determined individuals. To overcome these internal obstacles, it's crucial to cultivate self-awareness and self-confidence.

Start by challenging your negative thoughts and beliefs. Recognize that everyone faces moments of doubt and fear, but they don't have to define your journey. Surround yourself with a support system that believes in your abilities and encourages you to persevere.

2. Financial Constraints

Money is often a significant obstacle when chasing your dreams. Whether you dream of starting your own business, pursuing higher education, or traveling the world, financial constraints can seem insurmountable.

However, there are ways to work around this obstacle.

Create a realistic budget and savings plan to accumulate the funds needed for your dream gradually. Explore scholarship opportunities, grants, or financial aid programs that may help you achieve your goals. Consider part-time work or side gigs to supplement your income while pursuing your dreams.

3. External Challenges

Life has a way of throwing unexpected challenges our way, such as health issues, family responsibilities, or unexpected job changes. These external obstacles can disrupt your plans, but they don't have to derail them entirely.

Flexibility and adaptability are essential when dealing with external challenges. Be willing to adjust your timeline or approach to accommodate these unexpected events. Seek support from friends, family, or professionals who can help you navigate these difficult circumstances while moving forward.

Embracing Change

Change is an inevitable part of life, especially when pursuing your dreams. Your goals and aspirations may evolve over time, and external circumstances can shift unexpectedly. Embracing change means staying open-minded and adaptable throughout your journey.

1. Re-evaluating Your Goals

As you progress toward your dreams, it's essential to reassess your goals periodically. Are they still aligned with your passions and values? Have new opportunities or interests emerged? Be willing to adjust your goals if necessary to ensure they continue to reflect your true desires.

2. Learning from Setbacks

Setbacks and failures are not the end of the road; they are valuable learning experiences. Instead of viewing them as obstacles, see them as opportunities for growth. Analyze what went wrong, identify the lessons learned, and use that knowledge to improve and move forward.

3. Staying Adaptable

The world is constantly changing, and your journey may take unexpected turns. Embrace these shifts as opportunities rather than setbacks. Adaptability is a valuable skill that allows you to pivot when necessary, seize new opportunities, and continue moving toward your dreams.

In the pursuit of your dreams, obstacles and change are inevitable. However, they are not roadblocks but stepping stones on your path to success. By identifying and overcoming obstacles and embracing change, you'll reach your destination and become stronger and more resilient. Remember that your dreams are worth the effort, and the journey is a valuable part of the experience.

CHAPTER 4

Seanathan Polidore

Chapter 4

Harnessing Your Creativity and Innovation

By Seanathan Polidore

"You must be willing to stumble and trip many times in order to fall upon something great." - Sean P.

In chapter two, I spoke to you about how to take your dream from your mind and put it on paper so you can make it tangible. Now, I want to talk about you harnessing and honing your craft. My first suggestion I have for you in harnessing your creativity is focusing on the environments you place yourself in. From my experience as a six-year online college student, fitness coach, and now a writer, I can say that all of these endeavors can be done by yourself in the comfort of your own home if you so choose. But the odd part about it is that Most people struggle to actually reach their peak fitness at home, for example. There are tons of fitness content all over the internet and television. With this at-home program and that home-at supplement, the fitness world is literally a multi-billion-dollar industry. Yet, the truth of the matter is MOST people buy these programs, apps, and equipment and barely ever touch them more than three times before they stack laundry on top of their fine machinery (This is how I was able to outfit my entire gym when I started one, a lesson for another day.) When a person changes their clothes into workout attire, drives to the physical location, and gets inside a building full of people trying to change themselves, that person has an incredibly higher percentage of success than being at home. What was the difference, you may ask? Environment!

Put Your Face In the Place

One of the major keys to building your creativity will be placing yourself in spaces where others are creating, even if it's not in your particular field of practice. Just being around other people who are driven, focused, and have a dream, too, will stoke some of the fire inside your heart. Observing how other creatives operate, their small, nuanced habits, the discipline they possess, the passion they pour into their subject matter, and how they speak highly about it as if it's the most precious thing in the world. All these things can help you fine-tune and get the wheels turning in your own creative endeavors. Another advantage of being in the right environment is that it naturally makes you want to get moving instead of wasting time procrastinating or being distracted by your smartphone. The reason why so many people struggle with online schooling and home workouts is not because they lack the ability to do it but because it is very hard to be disciplined on your own. You can have all the best intentions in the world; everything around us these days is created to grab our attention on purpose. If you are a writer and you put yourself inside a bustling coffee shop or library where other people are at their tables pounding away at their laptops, working and studying, something inside of you says, let me put this phone down and get some words on the page. Even if you don't walk over and talk to these people (in fact, don't do that), just seeing them in the environment will jumpstart your desire to work as well. The same holds true for my gym example earlier; if people are around, you working hard, sweating, giving it their all every set, something inside of you says damn that, I'm over here working hard as well! I want to add that I think because of the pandemic in 2020, more people are inclined to want to stay in their cozy and comfy homes and try to do as many things online as possible. You can stream concerts, games, and movies. You can take classes and attend book signing. I mean, the sky is really the limit these days, but there is something special about taking the gas money, buying the flight, getting the hotel, paying for the event, and actually being in people's physical presence that A.I. has NOT figured out just yet. In today's society, we underestimate the power of physical touch. Shaking hands, exchanging hugs and embraces, sitting with others, and exchanging ideas. In the old Star Trek TV series, they had something called a Mind Melt. Have you ever been so engaged with someone in a conversation that it's as if your brains are synced together? That is the type of connection that we are missing today, and a great deal of creative juice is going untapped because of it.

Like Attracts Like

For some people, the spaces you are in daily may not have another person even close to your interest in it. Placing yourself in the right environment for your dreams will narrow down the process of finding instructors, teachers, and mentors because you will greatly increase the percentage of people who care about the same things you value and care about. While you are there, seek out those who seem further along in their process than you. Learn to be curious as a five-year-old child again. Ask a lot of questions. Try to exchange contact information if you can and find creative ways to pick their brain about what they are doing and, at the same time, share with them what you are attempting to do. Also, besides trying to find advanced people to help your journey, look to younger people behind you who may be in earlier stages than you are. Try to assist them in any way possible and offer to coach them up. One of my favorite sayings is, "To teach is to learn twice." As you are guiding them and explaining concepts to them, you are deepening the understanding inside of yourself, but you may also see something in a brand-new light from their fresh eyes point of view that you may not have ever stumbled upon on your own. Being around youthful energy can also be very inspiring and motivating for an older creative person because the younger crowd tends to throw caution to the wind and take more risks than a lot of older people because, at that point in life, they have a lot less to lose. They most likely don't have children and a spouse yet; they don't have a home to pay for and other parts of life that are beautiful indeed, but subconsciously, it can make you not take as many chances. The idea I try to have in mind is to keep people in my life five to ten years older than me and also keep people in my circle who are five to ten years behind me. I try to remain the link in between. Concepts like this help me to streamline my process and accelerate my learning in a few different areas of my life.

Keep Yourself Open To New Experiences

This one principle may be the hardest to apply out of this entire publication. It will be the hardest because, naturally, we are creatures of habit, and we can be very stuck in how we are used to doing things. When you are on your journey to hone your creativity, you must be a blank canvas waiting to be painted on. You have to experience life like a baby all over again as if you have no understanding of what is happening around you and are just ready to soak it all in. If you are a parent or have been around small kids, you may remember a phase when all you heard was, why this, what's that, who's that, why that way, why that order? Why can't I do it this way, etc? We have to really go back to thinking of life that way again to soak up creative possibilities in what we are seeing, hearing, and experiencing in life. Allow yourself to go to restaurants you would never usually go to, or if you go to a tried-and-true spot, order something you would never order. Make yourself watch a few T.V. shows and movies you would not watch regularly. On a day off, drive to different parts of your city you would never venture out into or drive to a new city. All of these types of examples and more are ways to open up new pathways in your mind. Give yourself a new taste to describe in your writing, new colors to use in your painting, and new textures to play with in your clothes design. If you do what you always do, you will get what you always get. It's true! You must be exposed to new things to create new things. Have you noticed how some of your favorite rappers, as they get some money and tour the country and the world, their topics start to change? How they dress and how they vacation and spend their time evolves because they have been exposed to brand new parts of the same life they always had.

Give and GO!

The thing I will share on harnessing your creativity is finding a place to share your craft. Now, this book is not just for writers; creativity comes in many forms, and the principles in this publication can be used by anyone, which is the intent. I have observed that when it comes to creatives, they will usually tell you that they create what they do for themselves and they are not lying. To a large degree, we get so many things out of the creation process that greatly improve our daily lives, but at the end of the day, most art is made to be seen or heard by someone outside of ourselves. I find the more you find spaces to share your art and get feedback, the more it helps to stoke more creative confidence and juice to flow. Confidence is such a crucial part of being a dreamer and a visionary. You must have an almost absurd belief in yourself and that your idea can work. As Kofi said in the beginning, there will be more naysayers than cheerleaders. You will need the confidence to press forward and push past any doubts from the outside, but more importantly, from yourself. Sharing your work with others and letting them critique your work, give suggestions, or tell you how much they enjoyed it gives you what they call in the business world "proof of product." You have hard evidence that you have some future in this thing, but only if you keep applying yourself and putting more time into practicing your skills.

I love to give working examples to highlight my principles when I write. For this section, I will speak on my experiences as a new person in the world of poetry and the spoken word. During the pandemic, I decided to learn some new skills, and along with that came the desire to get into the world of poetry. In true Sean P. fashion, I go on Instagram and start to follow and befriend seasoned poets in the space. Before long, we were exchanging pieces with each other and bouncing ideas off of one another to sharpen our skills. Over time, I gained enough courage to attend some local poet and spoken word events. Most times in these events, the poets taking the stage have spent many years in that setting. They are used to the order of things and the rules of engagement, and they most likely know every person in the room. They are at home for the most part. When I started going into these rooms and performing my private pieces to a crowd of strangers and getting their reactions in real-time, it greatly improved my confidence in what I was doing, but it also helped me to sharpen how I go about creating future pieces. When you share your work with others, you realize the large gulf between what sounds and looks good to you in private versus when you are actually performing it or showing something that doesn't work as well. You would never know something like that unless you have the courage to let others see and comment on your work. Once I had seasoned veterans coming to me afterward saying what they loved and saying some of my words back to me, it gave me a boost that I will take in my writing going forward.

CHAPTER 5

Dr. Ashley Wade

Chapter 5

"Building Resilience and Persistence"

By Dr. Ashley Wade

Focus on developing the resilience and persistence needed to keep moving forward in the face of setbacks and failures, emphasizing the importance of perseverance.

Welcome to the next stage in your process. As a scientist, I've come to appreciate stages and processes. Resilience is a personal quality that ultimately keeps you grounded because you will need to rely on it as you grow and as your life changes. The truth is as you invest in your development, your personal and professional life will change, and you will go through different levels of elevation: mentally, physically, spiritually, and emotionally. According to the American Psychological Association, resilience is defined as "the process and outcome of successfully adapting to difficult or challenging life experiences, especially through emotional and behavioral flexibility and adjustment to external and internal demands." Pause. Ok, that was a mouthful. Look up these words: Adapt, Flexibility, and Adjustment. Right. As you can imagine, resilience is an important quality to Develop because life is a journey of continuous unfolding and continuous enlightenment if you don't allow the roadblocks and learning experiences to consume you. I want you to know that I am in no way saying that this is an easily attainable quality to obtain. There's a really neat quote in The Kolbrin Bible that I'll always refer to: "No life is without conflict." This simple yet powerful statement reminds us that each and every one of us has Conflict in our lives and Constant things to overcome. This may create some internal anxiety because, based on science, we seek homeostasis, which means balance or stability. That's why it's essential to read and invest in your personal development and add tools to your toolkit that you can use as obstacles arise because they Will. That's guaranteed. How we will handle the obstacles is the burning question. Having resilience requires that you Learn, Apply the lessons learned, and then focus on the future. The key to resilience is Learning and realizing that you are not Taught how to achieve this. We must read books and commit to being lifelong learners of psychology in some sense. We must learn about Ourselves and Allow ourselves to Develop. How can you move forward, onward, and upward? You must be your own leader first. Learn to trust yourself and trust that the Universe has your back and wants to see you be successful and happy in this life- conflict and all. One way you can honor the resilience you build along the way is by Creating. If you have an idea… then develop and execute it. Don't let yourself down. Don't give up. So many of us have "let down" stories where we have in some way been disappointed. Trust that your Spirit and Abilities will lead you in the right direction so You become someone You can Depend on. Build into your Resilience by being unstoppable. Do you believe that you are unstoppable? Oh, ok, then show me. Watch how much happier you become. Let the things that you create make you Proud. As you start to do these things, you will begin to see that you Can Persevere. Push forward. Don't allow the obstacles to stop you. That means you can keep going even in the face of difficulty. Now, this is different than being in survival mode. The difference is in how you handle the stress. Ponder on that. Ultimately, it literally takes you reminding yourself how important you are to the Universe. Your presence and the gifts that are within your purpose are necessary for the present and future. Not just for what you Can Do, but Who You are as a person. Develop this affirmation into your psyche. Believe it. Be Solid on this. Certain of it. In tough times, you'll need these Power statements to fuel your Resilience and Perseverance. Let's practice this together.

Be Great, Good People.

Sincerely,

Dr. Wade

CHAPTER 6

Dr. Ashley Wade

Chapter 6

Celebrating Success and Reflecting on the Journey

By Dr. Ashley Wade

This final chapter is about recognizing and celebrating the milestones achieved, reflecting on the growth and learning that occurred along the journey, and setting sights on future dreams and visions.

Yes! Listen. What I'm saying is that with an elevated mindset and the forward movement in your creations and personal development, you Will Accomplish your Goals. I mention the word creativity frequently because as you deposit knowledge and lessons into your personal psychology, you have to produce through your Unique energy. Whatever it is that you create, nobody can do it like You! Exactly! And honey, that deserves a celebration. Celebrations feel better when you know you have Earned them. Celebrate the achievements that you make. You'll move through celebrating your stages to Celebrating the finished products.

Hallelujah, somebody. Whew, I almost took off running. Celebrate completions. Celebrate the Partnerships and the Advances. The revenue. The new opportunities. You want to know why this is such an important step? Because folks give up on themselves every single day. Easy. So many of us live defeated. Folks will have a grand idea, then let the idea disappear, the dream fizzle, and they lose hope. Guess what… you didn't! That's noteworthy. That's worth more than a pat on the back. I can't tell you what exactly to do to celebrate because we all have different tastes but do it and make it special. Let your choice incorporate movement, dance, smiles, laughter… and Freedom. As you increase in your spiritual awareness of how things happen around you, you will see that as you begin to get in the flow, the Universe will put a little razzle on top of the steps you take, proving that you believe in yourself, which means that you Believe in the Creator(s). It's bigger than the thing. Celebrations demonstrate that you believe in Your spiritual Power and Manifest it through your physical person. The many parts of you working together to activate your Purpose(s) somehow make this world a better place.

And don't stop with one accomplishment. See, most people wait for the one big thing. The graduation, the degree, the promotion, the award. Although those are tremendous accomplishments, they are ones that you have to wait for someone else to give you. Create so that you can celebrate Frequently and Continuously. Give Yourself a Reason to Celebrate. Keep it going! Keep that Energy Up! Continue to seek Wisdom for your next Steps, Pay attention, and follow your Paths. Before you know it, you will have a whole new flow to your resume. The one idea manifested will turn into two, then three, and then… who knows what you will make of your life. There's so much more quality in this type of living. Maybe it's a little bit of this AND a little bit of that. Maybe the flow will have items directly related to your career choice, and maybe they won't. Remember, you are open and willing to utilize the fullness of your potential. Before you know it, you'll have surprised yourself at what all you can do. I know it to be True. That deserves a special acknowledgment, don't you think? Let this positive cycle inspire you to stay focused and productive with your ideas. Put it on paper. Execute the vision, and Celebrate the fact that You and the World are better because of the Seeds that you Sow. Our future relies on what you learn and what you create. What does your vision say? What do you see? What do you imagine? One creation at a time, we Will make this world a better place. We will Demonstrate to the world the Power of Melanin and why Cultured People are so important- By being exactly who we were created to be… in the fullness.

I am important, and You are Important. Let's Grow Together.

Sincerely,

Dr. Ashley Wade

Pharmacist, Author, Curator, Literacy and Community Advocate, Griotte.

CHAPTER 7

Kofi Piesie

Chapter 7

Steps by Step Dreams, Goals, and Action Plan

By Kofi Piesie

This section of the book will give you a step-by-step guide on how to turn your dreams and vision into goals, so let's get straight to it.

Step 1: Identifying Your Dreams and Visions

To translate your dreams and visions into goals, the first step is identifying what you really want. This requires being reflective of oneself and engaging in introspection. Spend some time reflecting on shared dreams and visions. What do you want to have in your personal life, working career, or relationships? What are your interests and passions?

When you identify your dreams and visions, write them down. This makes them vivid in your life without confusion. Remember, dreams and visions change with time; hence, they should be reviewed and updated regularly.

Step 2: Setting Specific and Measurable Goals

Having determined your dreams and vision, it is high time you formulated them into specific, measurable goals. The clear and self-explanatory goal cannot be confused with anything else, hence its specificity. Goals that can be measured imply quantifiability, that is, the point at which such a goal can be said to have or not, depending on the measurement criteria.

Use the SMART framework to help you set specific and measurable goals. The letters in its acronym stand for Specific, Measurable, Attainable, Relevant, and Time-bound. When you apply these criteria when setting your goals, they are bound to be realistic, achievable, and likely to strike a chord in matters of global visioning.

For example, if your dream is to set up your own business, then a SMART goal might be: "Over the next six months, I will develop and finalize a complete business plan and raise funds for my business idea."

Always remember that every goal must be specific, measurable, and time-bound to increase your chances for success.

Step Three: Breaking Down Your Goals into Action Plans

After setting your goals, the next thing is breaking your goals into small actionable steps. This makes your goals look easy and not overwhelming. Identify some of the major milestones or steps you will use to achieve each goal.

Next, break down each milestone into smaller tasks or actions. These tasks must be specific and actionable to enable you to progress toward your daily or weekly goals. This further increases your chances of success and completely eliminates the feeling of being overwhelmed when listing smaller steps, which will help break down each goal.

Step 4: Create a Timeline for Executing Your Goals

Develop a timeline for goal execution, with deadlines to go with each step or milestone along the way, making a schedule or a calendar.

It is a good way of adding a sense of urgency and setting priorities. It also helps you keep track of your progress, allowing you to make the necessary alterations if necessary. However, this never means that the timeline needs to be followed with absolute strictness; it must be flexible enough to deal with any eventualities or shifting of goals.

Step 5: Developing a Support System and Accountability

With goals, it is not a lonely journey. You have to develop a support system and mechanisms of accountability that make you remain focused and motivated throughout the period. Discuss your goals with some trusted friends, family members, or counselors and share with them your achievement paths.

Consider joining a mastermind group or looking for an accountability partner chasing the same goals. This will be of great help in giving you ideas, holding you accountable, and encouraging you on this amazing journey.

Step 6: Staying Motivated and Overcoming Challenges

In the course of actualizing your goals, realities for doubts about proceeding will be waiting for you. It would be best if you devised a plan to overcome such difficulties by ensuring that you stay motivated. One of the available strategies is breaking down your goals into defined and achievable steps.

Celebrate small wins that boost your motivation and confidence along the way. Connect with positive and inspiring people who uplift and encourage you. Look for resources, like books or podcasts, that offer inspiration and practical advice.

Remember, obstacles are all part of the process. Use them as opportunities to learn and grow, but don't lose sight of your overall goals and vision.

Conclusion

Achieving success entails turning one's dreams and, later, vision into goals. Following this simple procedure, you can turn your burning desires into something practical and actionable in a given time period. Remember to be focused, motivated, and flexible along the way. With determination and perseverance, you can make your dreams come true and achieve success.

ABOUT THE AUTHORS

Author Bio
Senathan Polidore

Mr. Seanathan Polidore is the son of Clarence and Versana Polidore. He is a year 2000 graduate of Franklin Senior High School. Mr. Polidore continued his education to earn a master's degree in psychology. His life has quite a few adventures. Some of those include the U.S. Navy, being a husband and father, health and fitness trainer, co-founder of Pen Business Solutions, motivational speaking for schools and community groups, and the author of five self-help books. You can find his author interviews on Instagram, where he has had the pleasure of interviewing a number of nationally recognized authors as well as him being interviewed. Mr. Polidore's mission in life is to get books into more hands and to leave everyone he meets with something to think about.

Author Bio

Kofi Piesie

Kofi Piesie is a Pan-African Lecturer and author and is a member of Seshew Maa Ny Medew Netcher, a group that studies Ancient Egyptian Writing and language, Mossi Warrior Clan; the group studies intensively in West Africa, and the Kofi Piesie Research Team that researches and studies African American and African history, culture, writing, and languages.

Kofi Piesie has been an independent researcher for 9 years and has been presenting information for 7 years using the ancient Egyptian word tp Hsb, which means the correct method. In 2013 he made it his mission to reconstruct the African Mind, and a few years later, he created a channel that takes the Eurocentric mind of the black man, woman, and child and Africanizes it, called Kofi Piesie TV, in 2017.

Kofi is the CEO and owner of Same Tree Different Branch Publishing, and the company provides a one-stop shop for authors, researchers, teachers, entrepreneurs, and business owners. The company prides itself on quality work and quick turn services.

Kofi Piesie is also the CEO and owner of Mboka-Famliy Connected Apparel—an online apparel company with brands representing African and African American culture.

Author Bio

Dr. Ashley Wade

Ashley Wade Pharm D is a Consultant Pharmacist from Longview, TX, currently living in Dallas. She is a knowledge enthusiast, conscious thinker, and motivational speaker. She is a healer who enjoys connecting with people spiritually to positively change their lives.

Ashley is also the author of "It's A Journey: A Holistic Journal for Discovering Self," where she created a process and safe space for those who are open to connecting with themselves on a deeper level.

Through her immense passion for reading and studying revolutionary pioneers and black philosophers, she has found a special connection between the inner self and divinity- this is the message she shares with those she encounters.

Dr. Wade enjoys creating unique learning experiences for people to explore historical non-fiction via her book club, and she really enjoys engaging in deep discussions with her friends.

Her belief is that self-discovery, awareness, and knowledge are power!

Her most recent publication is an article in Voyage Dallas Magazine and "The Modern-Day Griots and Griottes: The New Generations."

She started ADH Pharmacy Consulting, LLC in 2021, creating opportunities for people to ask questions and receive advice from a Licensed Pharmacist. Our services provide information about medication and chronic disease education while empowering patients to increase their healthcare knowledge and encouraging holistic lifestyle changes. Self-discovery coaching, journaling, study sessions, and book club curation are some of our other supporting services.

We believe in connecting our community with knowledge and kinetic energy. Special thanks to our community partners and supporters near and far.

https://www.sametreedifferentbranchpublishing.com/

Office: 601-695-5797

Email: labarracenelson@yahoo.com

www.ingramcontent.com/pod-product-compliance
Lightning Source LLC
Chambersburg PA
CBHW071223160426
43196CB00012B/2392